My Book about Brains, Change and Dementia

What is Dementia and What Does it Do?

Lynda Moore
Illustrated by George Haddon

Jessica Kingsley Publishers
London and Philadelphia

First edition published in hardback in Great Britain in 2018 by Jessica Kingsley Publishers
This paperback edition published in Great Britain in 2023 by Jessica Kingsley Publishers
An imprint of Hodder & Stoughton Ltd
An Hachette UK Company

1

A CIP catalogue record for this title is available from the
British Library and the Library of Congress

ISBN 978 1 83997 748 0
eISBN 978 1 78450 901 9

Printed and bound in Great Britain by Ashford Colour Press

Jessica Kingsley Publishers' policy is to use papers that are natural,
renewable and recyclable products and made from wood grown in
sustainable forests. The logging and manufacturing processes are expected
to conform to the environmental regulations of the country of origin.

Jessica Kingsley Publishers
Carmelite House
50 Victoria Embankment
London EC4Y 0DZ

www.jkp.com

For Alan Trengove, my close friend of many years,
outstanding achiever in sport, work and life in general.
A fine man of fine mind. I hold you in
mind in illustrating this book.

G.H.

Acknowledgements

This book was originally developed for Dementia Australia's 'Dementia in My Family' website project to provide resources for children and young people who have someone with dementia in their lives. Many people across the organisation contributed to this project and their work is greatly appreciated. In particular, Dementia Australia would like to acknowledge the members of the 'Dementia in My Family' team: Brighid Brodie, Heather Chapman, Lois Cyngler, Sophie Hennessey, Stroma Mauritzen, Lynda Moore and Ann Reilly. A special thank you to Stroma, for without her vision and commitment this book would not have moved from the e-world onto the shelves.

Further information about dementia and help for children of all ages and the adults supporting them can be found at www.dementiainmyfamily.org.au.

Dementia Australia extends a sincere thank you to George for his generosity, sensitivity and creativity. His adorable illustrations bring this book to life and add a very special kind of magic. Visit George's website at www.georgehaddon.com.au.

Guide for Grown-ups

It's great that you have chosen to read about dementia with your child. This book was designed as a way of starting up the conversation between you. Be ready for your child to ask questions that might surprise you! We hope this book helps you feel more confident to answer them.

The words and subject matter have been carefully chosen by Dementia Australia's family counsellors. They offer one way of explaining complex concepts such as brain function, dementia progression and death, as well as exploring a child's feelings about these things. In this way, this book caters to children who have a loved one at any stage of the disease. Although difficult, many parents find it helpful to have honest conversations with children (of any age) about the realities of dementia because:

- it enables the child to make sense of what they have already noticed going on around them

- the reality can be less frightening for a child than the unknown

- it opens the door for them to share their fears, worries and questions with you

- it allows them to adjust to and prepare for what is to come

- it gives them permission to discuss difficult subjects with you.

That being said, each child and family context is unique, so this book offers children control over when they choose to read about the end stages of dementia and death. They can opt to skip those pages if they are not feeling ready.

This is not a typical story book; the ending is a question for you and your child to ponder together.

Arms, tummy, legs, feet, toes,
fingers, hands, neck...HEAD!

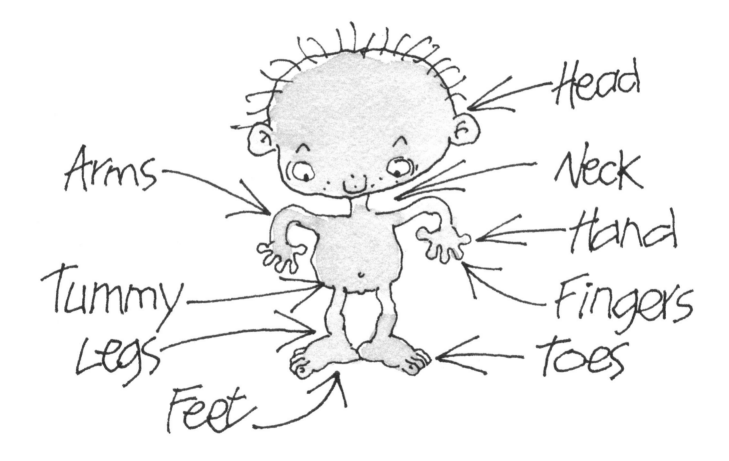

BUT…what's INSIDE our head?

A brain!

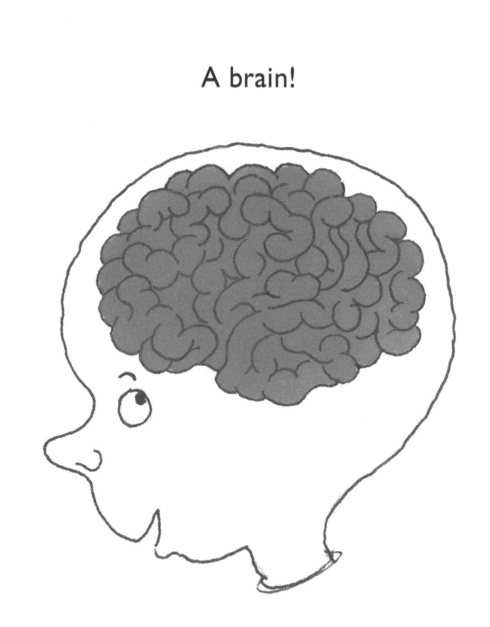

All of us have a brain in our head.

Animals have brains too.

Our brain is AMAZING!

It drives our body a bit like
a person drives a car.

Our brain drives our body
so we can do the things we do.

It makes our arms and legs move…

...and our mouth chew.

It makes us sleepy when we need to rest.

It lets us feel angry...or sad...
and makes us smile when we're happy!

We need our brain to do
EVERY SINGLE thing.

The trouble is, different parts of our body can get hurt or sick.

Brains can get sick too.

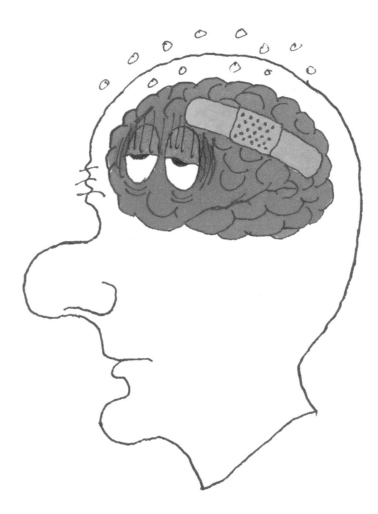

Sometimes, a person's brain gets sick with a disease called dementia.

Dementia has other names too – big long names that can be hard to remember.

Alzheimer's disease

[ahlts-hahy-merz] [dih-zeez]

Lewy body disease

Frontotemporal dementia

[fruhnt-o-tem-per-*uh*-l] [dih-men-sh*uh*]

Vascular dementia

[vas-ky*uh*-ler] [dih-men-sh*uh*]

When someone has dementia, it's as if their brain can't drive their body well anymore.

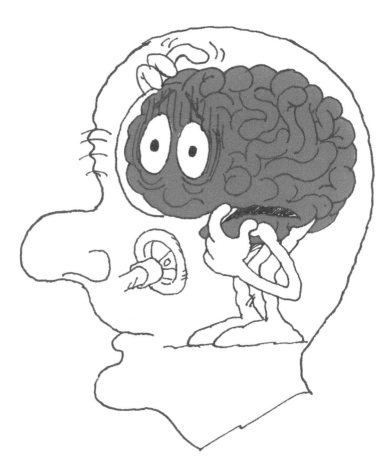

And the trouble is, we need our brain
to do every single thing.

So, when someone has dementia,
they might…

…need help with shopping or dressing…

...stop playing with you...

…feel bad, sad or angry more often…

...have trouble remembering things...

...or they might not!

But a person with dementia
WILL change in lots of different ways.

This is not their fault.
It's not your fault.
It isn't anybody's fault.
It's just the way
it is with dementia.

Usually, when we're sick, we get better. The trouble is, when someone has dementia, they won't get better.

None of the doctors in the world know how to make someone with dementia better.

But doctors, nurses, friends and family
can all help make sure people with
dementia have what they need.
Kids and pets can help too!

As time goes on, a person with dementia will need more and more help.

And the people looking after the person
with dementia will get busier!

Are you ready to read about what happens in the end when a person has dementia?

Take your time to answer this question.

If you're not ready, that's fine, just skip pages 32 and 33.

After a long time, dementia will make the person's brain so sick that it can't keep them alive anymore. When this happens, the person with dementia will die.

Have you ever talked about dying before?

Dying is a part of life. Dying is what happens
to every living thing at the end of its life.

It can be hard when someone you
know has dementia.

Sometimes you might feel…

happy…

or sad…

scared…

or really, really mad.

It's OK to have these feelings.

It can help to share our feelings.
When you're happy…or sad, scared…or mad,
who can YOU tell?

And what else helps
you feel better?